Backyard
Bugs
& Creepy-
Crawlies

Centipedes

Ashley Lee

Explore other books at:
WWW.ENGAGEBOOKS.COM

VANCOUVER, B.C.

e→ WWW.ENGAGEBOOKS.COM

Centipedes: Level 1
Backyard Bugs & Creepy Crawlies
Lee, Ashley 1995 –
Text © 2022 Engage Books
Design © 2022 Engage Books

Edited by: A.R. Roumanis

Text set in Epilogue

FIRST EDITION / FIRST PRINTING

LIBRARY AND ARCHIVES CANADA CATALOGUING IN PUBLICATION

Title: Centipedes / Ashley Lee.
Names: Lee, Ashley, author.
Description: Series statement: Backyard bugs & creepy-crawlies
Engaging readers: level 1, beginner.

Identifiers: Canadiana (print) 20250448542 | Canadiana (ebook) 20250448569
ISBN 978-1-77878-704-1 (hardcover)
ISBN 978-1-77878-713-3 (softcover)

Subjects:
LCSH: Centipedes—Juvenile literature.

Classification: LCC QL737.P94 C38 2025 | DDC J599.885—DC23

This project has been made possible in part by the Government of Canada.

Canada

Contents

What Are Centipedes?

Centipedes are not bugs. They are chilopoda (ky-LOP-uh-dah).

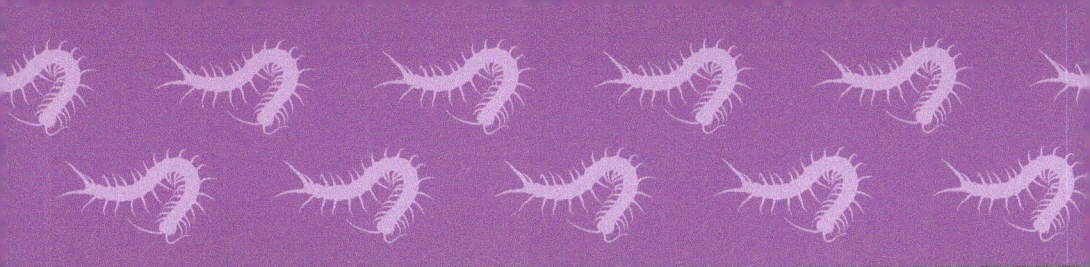

Scientists know of about 3,000 kinds of centipedes. They think there might be about 8,000 kinds.

What Do Centipedes Look Like?

Centipedes are split into pieces called segments. These segments make up a long, flat body.

Centipedes have hard exoskeletons. An exoskeleton is like a skeleton on the outside of the body.

6

Centipedes have at least 30 legs. Some have almost 400 legs!

Their front legs are also their fangs. They have **venom** in them.

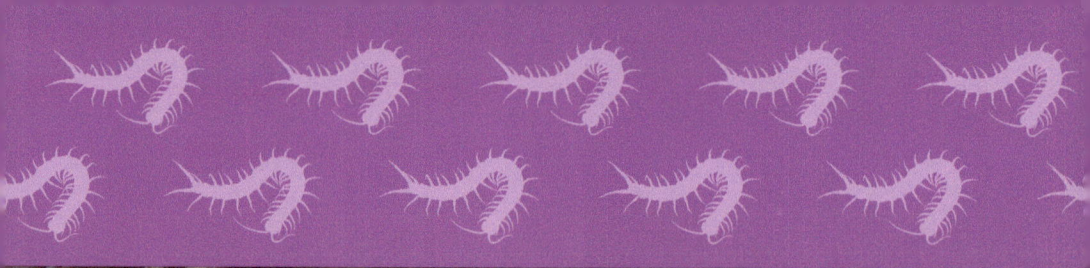

Where Do Centipedes Live?

Centipedes live all over the world. Many live in places that are wet so they do not dry out.

Most centipedes live in the soil or under rocks or leaves. Some centipedes live inside.

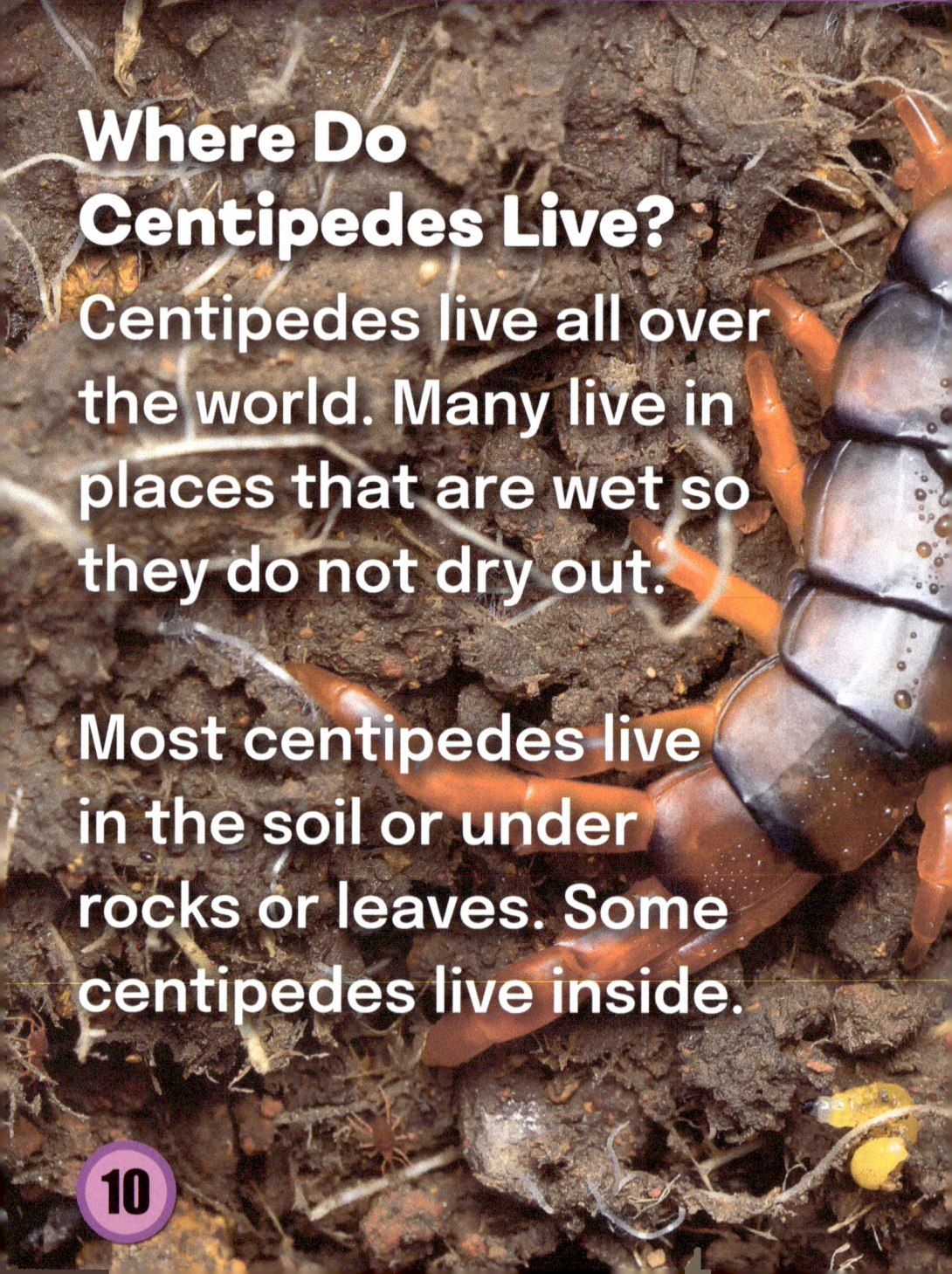

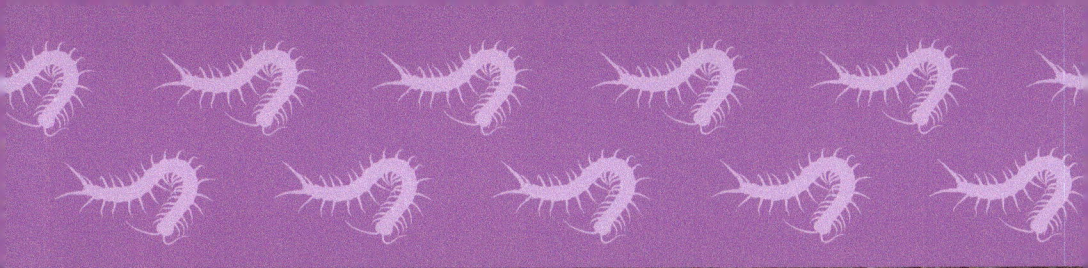

What Do Centipedes Eat?

Most centipedes eat any small creature they can catch. They like bugs, spiders, and worms.

Some bigger centipedes eat small animals. They may eat small lizards or birds.

12

13

Centipedes cannot see very well. They use their feelers to find food.

Centipedes use their venom to stop their **prey** from getting away.

14

Centipede Behavior

Centipedes hide during the day. They hide under rocks or leaves or in soil.

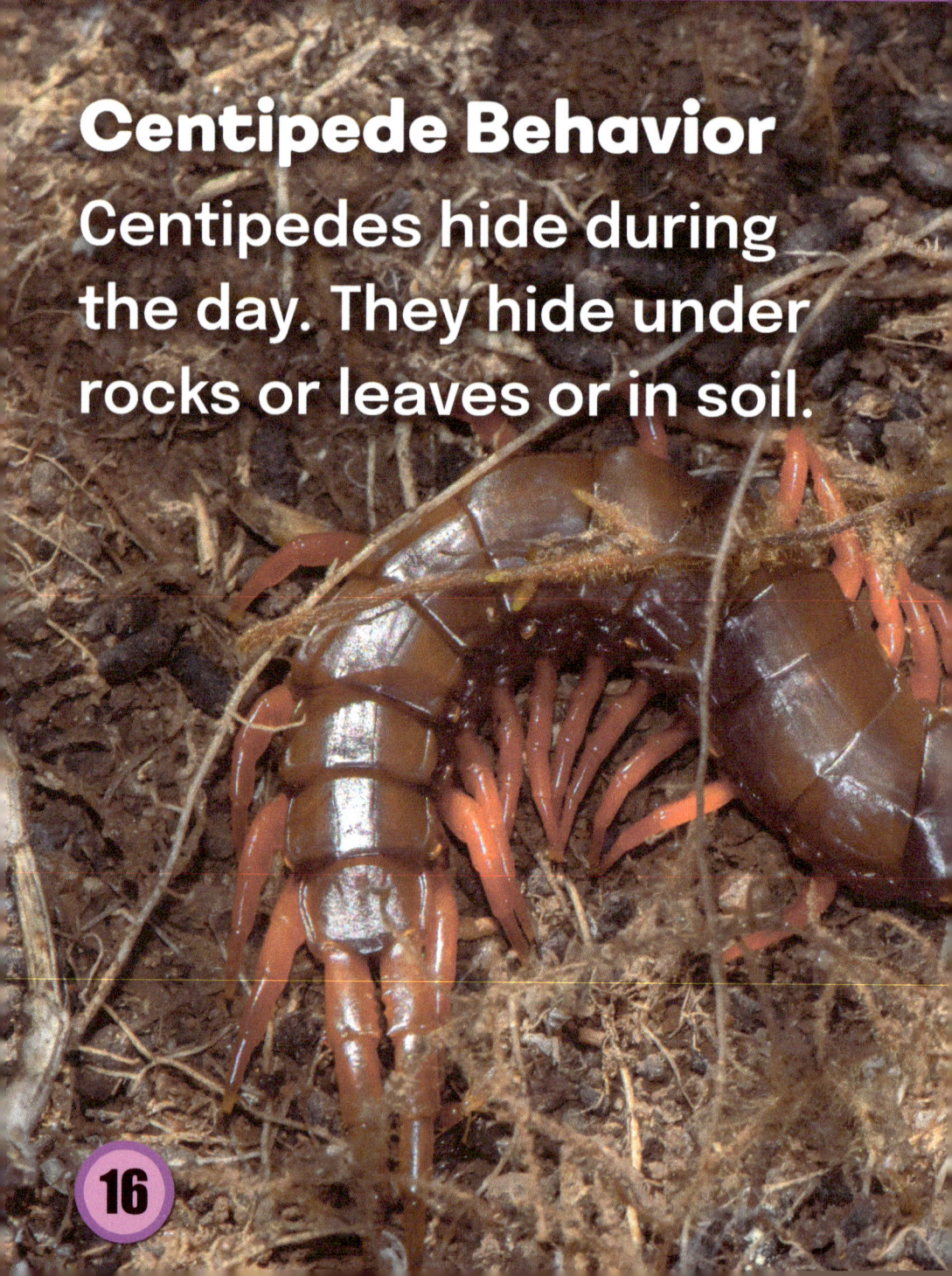

They are often more active at night. They leave their hiding places to hunt for food.

Centipedes often live alone. They are not often found in groups.

Centipedes are eaten by bigger animals. They can **detach** their leg if another animal grabs it. They can then grow a new one later.

Key Word

Detach: remove or take off.

18

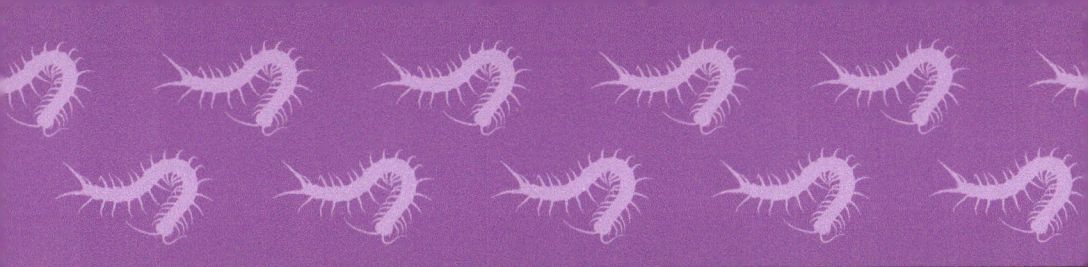

19

Centipede Life Cycle

Most female centipedes lay eggs in soil. They may curl around them to protect them.

Some centipedes give birth to live babies. Baby centipedes look like small adults.

Babies may not have all their legs at birth. They shed their skin to grow more legs and get bigger.

Most centipedes live for three to seven years. Some live for more than 10 years.

Fun Facts

Most centipede venom is not dangerous to people. It might still hurt if they bite though!

Centipedes have one pair of legs for each body segment.

"Centipede" means 100 legs. But centipedes cannot have exactly 100 legs.

Centipedes always have an odd number of leg pairs.

Are Centipedes Helpful or Harmful?

Centipedes are helpful! They dig tunnels in the soil. Tunnels help water get into the soil so plants can grow.

They also eat the bugs that harm gardens. This helps keep gardens safe.

Are Centipedes in Danger?

Many kinds of centipedes are not in danger. There are lots of them left.

Some kinds of centipedes are in danger. There are only a few left.

Quiz

Test your knowledge of centipedes by answering the following questions. The questions are based on what you have read in this book. The answers are listed on the bottom of the next page.

1 Are centipedes bugs?

2 Are a centipede's front legs also their fangs?

3 Do some centipedes live inside?

4 Do centipedes hide during the day?

5 Are centipedes often found in groups?

6 Can centipedes have exactly 100 legs?

Explore other books in the
Backyard Bugs & Creepy Crawlies series!

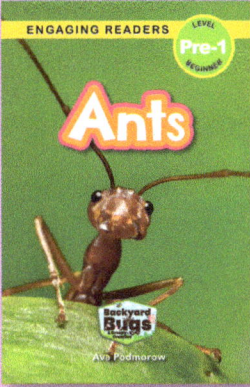

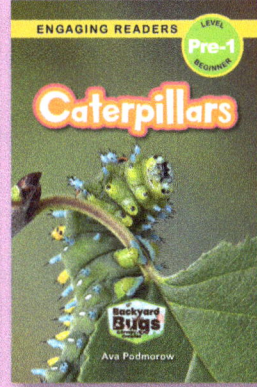

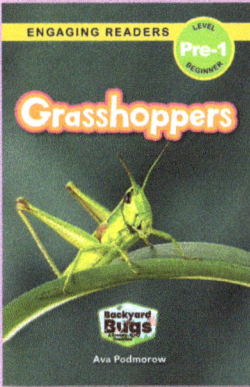

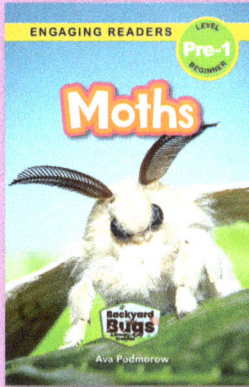

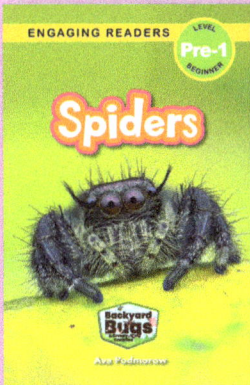

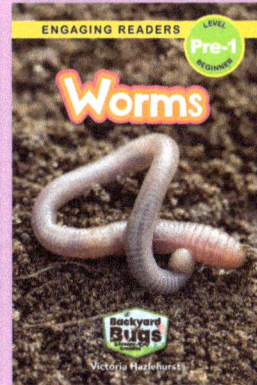

ENGAGING READERS — LEVEL Pre-1 BEGINNER

Ants
Backyard Bugs
Ava Podmorow

Beetles
Backyard Bugs
Victoria Hazlehurst

Caterpillars
Backyard Bugs
Ava Podmorow

Grasshoppers
Backyard Bugs
Ava Podmorow

Moths
Backyard Bugs
Ava Podmorow

Snails
Backyard Bugs
Ava Podmorow

Spiders
Backyard Bugs
Ava Podmorow

Wasps
Backyard Bugs
Sarah Harvey

Worms
Backyard Bugs
Victoria Hazlehurst

Visit www.engagebooks.com to explore more Engaging Readers.

www.ingramcontent.com/pod-product-compliance
Lightning Source LLC
Chambersburg PA
CBHW052035030426
42337CB00027B/5012